TO: _____

FROM: _____

DATE: _____

MESSAGE: _____

_____

_____

_____

Shop our other books at
www.sillyslothpress.com

For questions and customer service, email us at
support@sillyslothpress.com

JOKE 1

Two donkeys are considering crossing a road.

One says, "No way. Look at what happened to the zebra!"

JOKE 2

Q: What is faster- hot or cold?

A: Hot! Why? Because you can catch a cold!

JOKE 3

Have I told you about the time my dog ate the Scrabble tiles?

He kept leaving me little messages all around the house!

JOKE 4

Q: What does a baby computer call its father?

A: Data.

JOKE 5

Q: Why was the arena so windy?

A: It was full of fans.

JOKE 6

What did the goose say when she bought lipstick?

Put it on my bill

Daughter: Dad, I'm hungry!

Dad: Hi Hungry, I'm Dad.

Q: What did the buffalo say when his son left?

A: Bison!

Q: Why are doctors so calm?

A: Because they have a lot of patients.

JOKE 10

If two vegetarians get into a brawl, is it still considered a beef?

JOKE 11

Whoever invented AutoCorrect is a masshole.

He can duck right off.

JOKE 12

Q: Why is the bank so bad at keeping secrets?

A: Because it has so many tellers.

Q: What do you call a baby monkey?

A: A chimp off the old block.

Interviewer: Ok, so where do you see yourself in five years?

Applicant: Personally, I think my biggest flaw is listening.

My daughter asked, "Can I have a bookmark?"

I burst into tears.

12 years old and she still doesn't know my name is James!

JOKE 16

Wife: Honey, can you please put the cat out?

Husband: I didn't know it was on fire!

JOKE 17

Q: Have you heard about the pencil with two erasers?

A: It was pointless.

JOKE 18

Q: What do you call a dairy cow during an earthquake?

A: Milkshake.

Q: What did the janitor say when he jumped out of the closet?

A: Supplies!

Q: What time did the dad go to the dentist?

A: Tooth hurt-y.

I have a serious elevator phobia.

So, I take steps to avoid them.

Q: What should you give a sick citrus tree?

A: Lemon-aid!

Q: Why were the kitchen utensils stuck together?

A: Because they were spooning.

What does it sound like when a cow breaks the sound barrier?

Cow-boom!

Guess what the painter does when the temperature drops.

He puts on another coat.

Q: Why did the worker get fired from the cranberry juice factory?

A: Lack of concentration.

Q: What do you call a dog that doesn't have legs?

A: Whatever you want, he's still not coming.

JOKE 28

Q: Why is 288 never mentioned?

A: It's two gross.

JOKE 29

Q: What kind of dinosaur loves naps?

A: Stega-snore-us.

JOKE 30

Q: Why did the can crusher quit his job?

A: Because it was soda pressing!

JOKE
31

I was fired from the bank today.

A woman asked me to check her balance, so I pushed her over.

JOKE
32

Q: What did the notepad say to the pencil?

A: You have a good point!

JOKE
33

Q: Why are basketball players difficult to dine with?

A: Because they are constantly dribbling.

Q: When is a door not really a door?

A: When it's ajar.

Q: Can February march?

A: Nope! But April may!

Q: What happens when you witness a shipwreck?

A: You let it sink in.

Q: What is brown and sticky?

A: A stick.

Q: What do you call an elephant that doesn't matter?

A: An irrelephant.

Q: Name a room with no doors that nobody can enter.

A: A mushroom!

Q: What is the loudest pet you can have?

A: A trum-pet.

What did the baseball cap say to the sombrero?

You stay here, I'll go on ahead

Q: What did the policeman say to his belly?

A: You're under a vest!

Q: Why was the traffic light embarrassed?

A: Because everyone watched her change!

I have a great joke about construction.

I'm still working on it.

Q: Why did the policeman smear peanut butter on the road?

A: To go with the traffic jam!

JOKE 46

Q: What did the pirate captain say on his 80th birthday?

A: Aye matey!

JOKE 47

I got some shoes from a drug dealer.

I have no idea what he laced them with, but I have been tripping all day!

JOKE 48

Having trouble sleeping? I recommend cutting the legs of your bed.

You will sleep deeper.

Q: Do you know the best way to make someone curious?

A: I'll tell you tomorrow!

Doctor: Your test results show that you will live to be 70.

Patient: But I just turned 70.

Doctor: I know, I told you to take better care of yourself!

Q: Why did the melons get married?

A: Because they cantaloupe.

Q: What do Santa's elves listen to as they work?

A: Wrap music.

Q: Why did the potato go to the dentist?

A: It needed a root canal.

Q: Have you heard about the campground fire?

A: It was in tents.

I thought about going on an all-cashew based diet.

But that is just nuts!

Q: Why did the invisible woman turn down the job?

A: She just couldn't see herself doing it.

Q: Why did the belt get arrested?

A: Because he held up a pair of pants.

Q: Why did the bicycle fall asleep?

A: It was two-tired.

I used to work in the shoe-repair business.

I had to quit because it was sole destroying!

Q: Why are fish so easy to weigh?

A: Because they come with their own scales!

Q: What kind of music do windmills like?

A: They are metal fans.

Wife: I'm addicted to Twitter!

Husband: Sorry, I don't follow.

Once I met a girl who had 12 nipples.

Sounds freaky, dozen tit.

Sundays are always a little depressing, but the day before is a sadder day.

I had a neck brace fitted years ago.

I have never looked back since!

I just wrote a book on reverse psychology.

Whatever you do, do *not* read it!

I don't trust stairs.

They are always up to something!

I left my ex-girlfriend because she was so obsessed with counting.

I wonder what she is up to now.

Q: Have you heard about corduroy pillows?

A: They are making headlines.

Q: What do politicians and dirty diapers have in common?

A: Both should be changed regularly, and for the same reason!

Q: Why are ghosts the worst liars?

A: Because you can see right through them.

Q: What does a spider bride wear on her big day?

A: A webbing dress.

Q: What do you call a fibbing kitty?

A: Feline.

Just as I suspected.

Someone has been adding fertilizer to my garden.

The plot thickens.

Q: Why did the mechanic run out of mufflers?

A: Because his supply was exhausted.

JOKE 76

Q: Why don't ghosts go trick or treating?

A: Because they have no body to go with.

JOKE 77

Q: Who invented the round table?

A: Sir Cumference!

JOKE 78

Q: How did the hipster drown?

A: Mainstream.

Q: Where do fish deposit their money?

A: In a riverbank.

Q: Why can't you trust balloons?

A: Because they are full of hot air.

Q: What type of tea is the hardest to swallow?

A: Reality.

Q: What do you get a man with the heart of a lion?

A: Banned from the zoo.

Q: What do hillbillies drink from?

A: Hiccups.

Q: What happens when you cross a great white and a dog?

A: A terrified mailman.

Q: What is one of the worst things about being lonely?

A: Playing Frisbee.

Q: What does a stopwatch do when its hungry?

A: It goes back four seconds!

Q: What did the floor say to the wall?

A: Meet me at the corner.

JOKE 88

Q: What did the pillow say when it fell off the bed?

A: Oh sheet!

JOKE 89

Q: What did the mime say to his audience?

A: Nothing.

JOKE 90

Q: Why was Cinderella cut from the baseball team?

A: Because she ran away from the ball.

JOKE 91

Q: Why did the bank get bored?

A: Because it lost interest.

JOKE 92

Q: Where does steak go to dance?

A: The meat-ball.

JOKE 93

Q: How do you rob a snowman?

A: With a hairdryer.

Q: What gets wetter the more it dries?

A: A towel.

I have been considering taking up meditation.

It must be better than sitting around doing nothing.

Have you heard about the seamstress who fell into the upholstery machine?

She is fully recovered.

Name an animal that is always at a baseball game?

A bat.

Q: What does a house wear on a date?

A: Address.

Q: What is invisible and smells like worms?

A: A bird's fart.

JOKE 100

Q: What did the baby corn say when his dad went to work?

A: Where is popcorn?

JOKE 101

Q: What did the juicer say to the orange during quarantine?

A: I can't wait to squeeze you!

JOKE 102

Q: What did the Buddhist monk say at the hot dog stand?

A: Make me one with everything.

Kid: Dad, can you put my shoes on?

Dad: Nope, I don't think they will fit me!

Q: What do sea monsters eat for a snack?

A: Fish and ships.

Q: Where do baby cats learn how to swim?

A: The kitty pool.

Q: What do you call a guy with a rubber toe?

Q: Roberto.

Q: What happens when a frog's truck dies?

A: He gets a jump. And if that doesn't work, he has to get toad.

I broke my arm in two places.

My doctor told me to stop going to those places!

Q: Why are skunks romantic?

A: Because they are very scent-imental.

Q: How do bees style their hair?

A: With a honeycomb.

Q: Why are dogs such bad storytellers?

A: Because they only have one tale.

Son: I don't know, Dad. I just don't trust those trees over there.

Dad: Why that, Son?

Son: They look a bit shady!

Q: What do you call a sheep without legs?

A: A cloud.

I told my wife she drew on her eyebrows too high.

She seemed surprised.

Q: Why do fish live in salt water?

A: Because pepper makes them sneeze!

I could tell a joke about macaroni.

But it's a little cheesy.

Q: How can a cheetah change his spots?

A: By moving.

JOKE 118

Talking parrot for sale!

Because yesterday the little guy tried to sell me!

JOKE 119

Q: Why was it rude for a snowman to pick a carrot?

A: Because he was picking his nose!

JOKE 120

Q: Why did the scarecrow get an award?

A: He was outstanding in his field.

JOKE 121

Q: What kind of tree fits in your hand?

A: A palm tree!

JOKE 122

Q: Do you know the least spoken language in the entire world?

A: Sign language.

JOKE 123

Q: Why do ghosts ride in elevators?

A: Because it lifts their spirits.

Q: What do you call a
mountain who wants to
be a comedian?

A: Hill-arious.

Q: Did you hear about
the claustrophobic
supernova?

A: It really needed some
space.

Q: Why are space rocks
more delicious than
earth rocks?

A: Because they are meteor.

JOKE 127

Don't worry, you aren't completely useless.

You can always serve as a bad example.

JOKE 128

Q: How do snails fight?

A: They slug it out.

JOKE 129

Q: What do you call a belt made of clocks?

A: A waist of time.

JOKE 130

Q: How do you make a tissue dance?

A: Put a little boogie in it!

JOKE 131

Yesterday my wife asked me for some lipstick.

I accidently gave her a glue stick and she still isn't talking to me.

JOKE 132

What do you call a fish with one eye missing?

A f-shhh

Q: Why did the bank robber hide his money in the freezer?

A: He wanted cold hard cash.

Q: What is green and has claws?

A: Broccoli. I lied about the claws.

What did one pickle say to the other pickle?

Dill with it.

Q: How many tickles does it take to make an octopus laugh?

A: Ten tickles.

Q: How do meteorologists reach the top of a mountain?

A: They climate.

Q: What did the left eye say to the right?

A: Between you and me, something smells!

Q: Why are pigs bad at keeping secrets?

A: Because they squeal.

Q: Why don't you ever see hippos hiding in trees?

A: Because they are exceptionally good at it!

One company owner is talking with another.

"How do you get all of your employees to work on time?"

"It's easy! 40 employees, 30 parking spaces!"

Not to brag, but I finished the puzzle in a week.

It says 2-4 years on the box.

Q: How do attorneys say goodbye?

A: "We'll be suing you!"

Q: Why did the orange lose the race?

A: It ran out of juice.

Q: What do you call a dead almond?

A: Diamond.

Q: Why do you carry so much loose change?

A: No one can say I lack common sense.

Q: What should an alcoholic bird do?

A: Go to tweetment.

Q: What is the best way to impress a squirrel?

A: Act like a nut.

Q: What is at the bottom of the ocean and always shivering?

A: A nervous wreck.

Q: What do you call an alligator who wears a vest and fights crime?

A: An investigator.

Q: Why can't a hand be 12 inches long?

A: Because then it would be a foot.

Q: Do you know how popular that cemetery is?

A: People are just dying to get in there!

Q: What did the underwear say to the trousers?

A: What's up britches?!

JOKE 154

Q: What is the all-time number one cause of divorce?

A: Marriage.

JOKE 155

Oh man, I can't believe I forgot to go to the gym today!

That's 8 years in a row!

JOKE 156

Q: I have eighteen eyes, twenty teeth, and a very long nose. What am I?

A: Ugly.

Q: Which day do chickens dread?

A: Fri-day.

Q: What do you call someone with no body and no nose?

A: Nobody knows.

What do you call a sleeping bull?

A bull-dozer

Q: Which piece of school supplies is in charge?

A: The ruler.

Q: Why did the singer take a wheelbarrow to choir practice?

A: She needed something to carry a tune.

Q: What kind of shoes do bananas wear?

A: Slippers.

What do you call a karate move done by a pig?

A pork chop

I told my mother in law she had too much Botox.

She didn't seem surprised.

A wife caught her husband standing on a scale and sucking in his stomach. "That doesn't help," she said.

He replied, "Of course, it does! How else will I see the numbers?"

JOKE 166

Q: What is the most detail-oriented body of water?

A: The Pacific Ocean.

JOKE 167

My wife is always frustrated that I have no sense of direction.

So, I packed up my stuff and right.

JOKE 168

Q: What do you call a factory that sells passable products?

A: Satisfactory!

Q: What happens when you pamper a dairy cow?

A: Spoiled milk.

Patient: Hey doc, I am starting to forget things.

Doctor: When did it start?

Patient: When did what start?

Q: What has two butts and kills people?

A: An assassin.

Q: How much do pirates pay for corn on the cob?

A: A buccaneer.

The rotation of the earth really makes my day.

Q: Do you know what's up?

A: The sky.

Q: What is the best way to watch a fly-fishing tournament?

A: Live stream.

Q: What is a tornado's favorite game?

A: Twister!

I just started a book about anti-gravity.

It is impossible to put down!

JOKE 178

What did the soda can call his father?

Pop

JOKE 179

Stop looking for the perfect match. Just use a lighter.

JOKE 180

Q: What did the accountant say after a full day of work?

A: This is taxing!

The directions said, "Set the oven to 180 degrees."

Ok. But now I can't even open the door because it is facing the wall.

Q: Why did the teacher love her whiteboard?

A: Because it was just remarkable!

Q: Did I tell you about when I fell in love during a backflip?

A: I fell heels overhead!

JOKE 184

Justice is a dish that is best served cold.

If it were served warm, then it would be justwater.

JOKE 185

Gym Teacher's famous last word:

"All spears to me!"

JOKE 186

I told my PCP I heard buzzing.

He said, "It's just a bug going around."

I have heard that people pick their nose.

But I was just born with the one I have.

I started reading this horror story in Braille.

Something bad is going to happen. I can feel it.

Q: Have you heard about the math teacher who was afraid of negative numbers?

A: He would stop at nothing to avoid them!

Q: What do you call a dog magician?

A: A labracadabrador.

Q: Can a grasshopper jump higher than a house?

A: Of course! Houses can't jump.

I have this special talent. I can always guess what is inside a wrapped present.

It's a gift.

Q: Did you hear about the actress who fell through the floorboards?

A: She was going through a stage.

Q: What do you call a flower than runs on electricity?

A: A power plant.

Q: How do you keep a bagel from running away?

A: Lox it up.

Q: How do you know if there is an elephant under your bed?

A: Your head hits the ceiling!

Q: How does an Eskimo build a house?

A: Igloos it together.

Q: What kind of music do aliens listen to?

A: Nep-tunes.

If the early bird gets the worm, then I will sleep until there are waffles.

Have you heard about the naked woman who robs banks?

Nobody can remember her face!

Men 1820: I killed a buffalo.

Men 1920: I fixed the roof.

Men 2020: I shaved my legs.

Q: Where do crayons go to on vacation?

A: Color-ado.

Q: What is the best way to carve wood?

A: Whittle by whittle.

Q: Why did the jelly donut go to the dentist?

A: Because he lost his filling.

Q: What is the best way to communicate with a trout?

A: Drop it a line.

Q: Why do divers fall backwards off the boat?

A: Because if they fell forwards, they would still be on the boat!

Q: Why did the jellybean want to go to school?

A: To become a Smartie.

Have you heard about the bar on the moon?

Great drinks. No atmosphere!

Q: Why did the chef throw butter out of the window?

A: He wanted to see a butterfly.

Q: Why couldn't the delivery man mail any envelopes?

A: They were all stationary.

JOKE
211

Q: Why are piglets bad at sports?

A: Because they are always hogging the ball.

JOKE
212

Q: How do astronauts organize a surprise party?

A: They planet.

JOKE
213

I am just so good at sleeping.

I can do it with my eyes closed!

Q: Why was the chicken a bad referee?

A: He kept overcalling fowls.

Someone just threw milk at me. How dairy?!

Q: What did Adam say to his wife the day before Christmas?

A: It's Christmas, Eve!

Q: Have you heard the rumor about jelly?

A: Well, I'm not going to spread it!

Q: Do you know what really makes me smile?

A: My facial muscles.

Q: What time is it when a clock strikes 13?

A: Time to get a new clock!

Q: What do ghouls eat for dessert?

A: I-Scream.

Q: Why was the nose mad at the finger?

A: Because he was always picking on him!

I got this new deodorant.

The instructions say, "Remove cap and push up bottom".

I can't really walk, but when I fart it smells great.

Q: What happened when the grape got squished?

A: He let out a little wine.

I know money can't buy you happiness.

But I would be a lot more comfortable crying in a new sports car than a bike!

Q: What did the fisherman say when he ate the clownfish?

A: That tasted a little funny.

Q: Want to hear a joke about crying?

A: Never mind. It's tearable.

Q: Where did the computer go dancing?

A: The disc-o!

Q: Why do seagulls fly over the sea?

A: Because if they flew over the bay then they would be bagels!

Q: What did the volcano say to his girlfriend?

A: I lava you!

Q: What did the tonsil say to the adenoid?

A: Get dressed, the doctor is taking us out!

Q: Why can't you hear a pterodactyl using the bathroom?

A: Because the 'P' is silent.

Son: I'll call you later.

Dad: Don't call me later, call me Dad!

Q: What do you call an incredibly old snowman?

A: Water.

I would avoid the sushi if I were you.

It's a little fishy.

Q: Joe has 20 candy bars. He eats 15. What does he have now?

A: Diabetes. Joe has diabetes.

Q: What is an astronaut's favorite part of a computer keyboard?

A: The space bar.

Q: Why was 6 afraid of 7?

A: Because 7-8-9.

Q: How do professional athletes stay cool?

A: They are always surrounded by fans.

Q: Why don't peppers have friends?

A: Because they get jalapeno business.

What vegetable does a sailor avoid at all costs?

Leek

JOKE
241

Q: What is the award
for being the best dental
hygienist?

A: A plaque.

JOKE
242

Doctor: Hello. Do you have
an eye problem?

Patient: Wow! Yes, how did you
know?

Doctor: Well you came in through
the window instead of the door.

JOKE
243

How does a mummy start a
letter?

Tomb it may concern...

Q: What kinds of pictures do oysters take?

A: Shellfies.

I finally decided to sell my vacuum cleaner.

It was just gathering dust!

Q: What is the best present ever?

A: A busted drum. You can't beat it!

Wow so much has changed since my girlfriend got pregnant.

For example- my name, address, and phone number!

I am only familiar with 25/26 letters of the alphabet.

I do not know why.

I did my best to catch the fog.

But I mist it.

Q: What do you call a bull with no legs?

A: Ground beef.

Q: What do you call a man whose briefcase is in a tree?

A: A branch manager.

Q: What is a tapestry maker's favorite dance move?

A: Cutting a rug.

I entered a pun contest.

I submitted ten, figuring at least one would win.

But no pun in ten did.

Q: What is the difference between a cat and a comma?

A: A cat has claws at the end of its paws. A comma has a pause at the end of its clause.

Hey Dad, did you get a haircut?

Nope! I got them ALL cut!

Q: What kind of shoes do ninjas wear?

A: Sneakers.

Q: What did the two pieces of bread say about their relationship?

A: It was loaf at first sight.

Wife: I am worried about my husband. After he finishes his coffee, he eats the mug. All that is left is the handle!

Doctor: How weird. The handle is the best part!

Q: What did the tea report to the police?

A: A mugging.

Q: Why did the cucumber blush?

A: Because he saw the salad dressing.

Q: Why is a calculator so reliable?

A: You can count on it!

Q: What did one marijuana plant say to the other?

A: Hey bud.

Q: What did the ring finger say to the pinky?

A: I'm in glove with you.

Q: Why are spiders so smart?

A: They have full access to the web.

Q: Why did the pro golfer need new socks?

A: Because he got a hole in one.

Q: What do you call a toothless panda?

A: A gummy bear.

Son: Dad, what is an alcoholic?

Dad: Do you see those 4 trees? An alcoholic would see 8.

Son: But there are only 2 trees.

To the person who broke my glasses:

I will find you. I have contacts.

Q: What do you call an undercover noodle?

A: An impasta.

Pro tip: Don't buy anything with Velcro.

It's a total rip-off!

"My wife suffers from a serious drinking problem."

"Is she an alcoholic?"

"No, but I am! But she is the one who suffers!"

A mother asked her son, "Billy, do you think I am a good mom?"

Son: "My name is Sam."

Q: How do you get a country girl's attention?

A: A tractor.

JOKE 274

Comic Sans and Times New Roman walk into a bar.

The bartender yells, "Get out of here! We don't serve your type!"

JOKE 275

Q: Why should you avoid eating a watch?

A: Because it's too time consuming.

JOKE 276

How can a scientist make sure her breath is fresh?

With experi-mints!

Doctor: You are morbidly obese.

Patient: I want a second opinion!

Doctor: No problem, you are also ugly.

Q: Why did the baby cookie start crying?

A: Because its parents were a wafer so long.

Q: What is it called when you cross a snowman with a vampire?

A: Frostbite.

Customer: I am outraged! There is a hair in my soup!

Waiter: At this price, what did you expect? A whole wig?

I used to hate facial hair.

But then it grew on me.

A laboring woman started shouting, "Shouldn't! Wouldn't! Can't! Don't!"

But the midwife wasn't worried. It was just contractions.

Q: Why are elevator jokes so hilarious?

A: They work on so many levels.

Q: What do you call a miniature pony with a sore throat?

A: A little hoarse.

Q: Why did the woman get fired from the calendar factory?

A: Because she took a few days off.

Son to Mom: The kids are laughing at me and saying my teeth are too long!

Mom to Son: Oh hush! Look now you have scratched the floor again!

Q: Why do geologists love their jobs?

A: They're never taken for granite.

What did the plate say to the cup?

Dinner is on me!

What do you call a droid that takes the scenic route?

R2 detour.

Q: Why did the singer go sailing?

A: She wanted to hit the high Cs.

Q: Why does Waldo love to wear stipes?

A: Because he can't stand to be spotted!

Q: Have you heard about the man who invented the knock knock joke?

A: He was given the no-bell prize.

Q: Where do cows go on a date?

A: The moo-vies.

Q: What do you call a blind deer?

A: No-eye-deer.

Q: What did the professor do with the report on cheese?

A: She grated it.

Don't worry if a bird poops on your head.

Be happy that dogs can't fly!

Q: Why are dinosaurs so quiet?

A: Because they are dead.

Q: How do writers say hello?

A: Hey, haven't we metaphor?

Q: What did the papa chimney say to the baby chimney?

A: You are too young to be smoking!

Q: What is the difference between a numerator and a denominator?

A: A short line. (Only a fraction of people will understand this).

Q: What did the mountain say to the bluff?

A: Hey Cliff!

Q: What is the most patriotic sport?

A: Flag football.

Q: What did one Dorito farmer say to the other?

A: Cool Ranch!

Q: What do you call a guy who is found lying on your doorstep?

A: Matt.

Q: What is the best thing to do when you see a spaceman?

A: Park in it!

Name a kind of water that can't freeze.

Hot water.

JOKE 307

Q: What is green, popular, and sings?

A: Elvis Parsley.

JOKE 308

I just saw the most emotional wedding.

Even the cakes were in tiers!

JOKE 309

Q: Why did the computer go to the hospital?

A: It came down with a virus.

Q: Why do actors say, "Break a leg?"

A: Because they are part of a cast.

Q: What do you call queso that doesn't belong to you?

A: Nacho cheese.

Q: Why did Adele cross the road?

A: To say hello from the other side.

Q: When does a joke become a dad joke?

A: When it becomes apparent.

How can you tell if the ocean is friendly?

It waves!

Q: What is a lazy person's favorite exercise?

A: Diddly squats!

How does the moon
cut his hair?

Eclipse it.

Patient: Hey doc, I am
so nervous! This is my
first surgery.

Doctor: Don't worry.
Mine too!

Q: Why is it difficult
to explain jokes to
kleptomaniacs?

A: Because they are always
taking things, literally.

I invented a new word.

Plagiarism!

Hostess: Sorry about your wait.

Dad: Are you saying that I'm fat?

What type of building has the most stories?

The library!

JOKE 322

Q: Why do male ants float?

A: Because they are buoy-ant.

JOKE 323

Two fish are in a tank.

One asks the other, "How the heck do you drive this thing?"

JOKE 324

Q: What does a marching band instructor brush his teeth with?

A: A tuba toothpaste.

Q: Where did the newlywed bunnies go after their wedding?

A: On a bunny-moon!

Q: What do you call a lamb dressed as a Rockstar for Halloween?

A: Baaaaaad to the bone.

Q: What do you call a group of disorganized felines?

A: Cat-tastrophe.

Q: Why was the algebra book depressed?

A: It was full of problems.

My wife screamed, "YOU HAVEN'T LISTENED TO ANYTHING I'VE SAID, HAVE YOU?!?"

What a strange way to start a conversation.

I don't play soccer because I'm good at it.

I just do it for the kicks.

Wife to mother: My husband is making me so mad! I am coming to live with you.

Mother to wife: No. He should pay for his mistakes! I am coming to live with you.

Q: What did one legume say to the other?

A: How you bean?

"Hey grandma, why don't you have life insurance?"

"So, you can truly be sad when I die!"

Q: What did the digital clock say to the grandfather clock?

A: Look! No hands!

Q: Why don't clams donate to charity?

A: Because they are shellfish.

Q: Why are there two doors on chicken coops?

A: Because if they had four doors, they would be chicken sedans.

Q: What is the best way to catch a bra?

A: With a booby trap.

Q: Why did the chimpanzee fall out of the tree?

A: It was dead.

Who is a ghost's true love?

His ghoul-friend.

JOKE 340

Q: Why did the photograph go to jail?

A: Because it was framed.

JOKE 341

My boss told me to have a nice day.

So, I went home.

JOKE 342

A famished termite walks into a bar.

He says, "Where is the bar tender?"

I was told I should write a book.

What a novel concept.

Q: Why don't ants ever get sick?

A: Because they have anty-bodies.

Q: How can you identify a dogwood tree?

A: From the bark.

Singing in the bathtub is fun until you get shampoo in your mouth.

Then it becomes a soap opera.

Q: Why did the paper towel roll downhill?

A: To get to the bottom.

If a toddler refuses to go to sleep, are they guilty of resisting a rest?

Q: What kind of car does a chicken drive?

A: A Yolkswagen.

My dog used to chase people on a bike all day.

It got so bad that I finally had to take his bike away!

I just hate it when people say age is just a number.

Age is clearly a word!

JOKE 352

Q: Why shouldn't eggs tell jokes?

A: They would crack themselves up!

JOKE 353

Q: How many apples grow on a tree?

A: All of them.

JOKE 354

Q: What do you call an American bee?

A: A USB.

Q: What happens when you have a bladder infection?

A: Urine trouble.

Q: What do elves learn in kindergarten?

A: The elf-abet.

Q: What do you call a blind dinosaur?

A: A do-you-think-he-saw-us.

Man: You are the most beautiful woman in the world!

Woman: Whatever, you are just trying to get me in bed.

Man: And smart, too!

Q: What is the best thing about living in Switzerland?

A: I have no idea! But the flag is a big plus!

Isn't it weird how plastic surgery used to be so taboo?

But now with Botox, no one raises an eyebrow!

Q: Why was the substitute teacher wearing sunglasses?

A: Because the students were so bright!

Q: How was the paint thief apprehended?

A: He was caught red handed.

How can you stop an astronaut's baby from crying?

You just rocket!

Q: What do you call a dangerous sun shower?

A: A rain of terror!

I splurged on an expensive new belt, but it doesn't fit.

What a waist.

Printed in Great Britain
by Amazon